17 & Life

Allen Callaci

with photographs by Buzzsaw

BAMBOO
DART
PRESS

LOS ANGELES † NEW YORK † LONDON † MELBOURNE

17 & Life by Allen Callaci

ISBN: 978-1-947240-18-6

eISBN: 978-1-947240-19-3

First Printing 2021

For information:

Bamboo Dart Press

chapbooks@bamboodartpress.com

Curated and operated by Dennis Callaci and Mark Givens

Bamboo Dart Press 008

Pelekinesis
www.pelekinesis.com

BAMBOO DART PRESS
www.bamboodartpress.com

SHRIMPER
www.shrimperrecords.com

To the memory of Anna Marie Bachoc

"Learning is Life"
quote etched above the entryway of Upland Junior High.

We don't move on. We move in circles with the remainders of the past following from behind like shadows lingering out from forever.

I was barefoot, gingerly peeling an orange and living a gloriously unremarkable latchkey kid existence in the middle-class lite suburb of Upland, California the day my adolescence expired. I was 17 years old. The decade plus that I'd spent in Upland had been years filled with soul crushing certainty: the sun would rise every morning, the cul-de-sac streetlights would slowly flicker to life every twilight and each and every May would bring the Gibson Senior Center's Butterfly Celebration, an educational children's event devoted to the short, fragile life cycle of the butterfly:

Egg.

Caterpillar.

Chrysalis.

Butterfly.

Although the Upland eco-system lacked the fluid poetry of the life cycle of a Monarch butterfly's it was just as cyclical. One supermarket chain would go under every nine months and be replaced by another chain nine months later. Day turns to night. Night turns to day. Vons turns to Ralphs. Ralphs turns to Stater

Brothers. Stater Brothers turns to Vons. Repeat ad nauseum.

The city had branded itself "The City of Gracious Living" in 1906 when it had changed its name from North Ontario to Upland. It was a name change that had been inspired by the Citrus growers who boasted that their citrus came from higher ground. Longtime locals sometimes referred to their city as "the city of gracious living" with a certain sense of communal pride and pre-eminence. Not me. Upland, to me, was a scratchy, mothball smelling blanket that I could not wait to crawl out from beneath. My plan was to tightly wrap myself in bubble-wrap made from the finest rock n roll and comic books until that day arrived.

"Did you know a girl named Anna Marie Bachoc?" my mom asked in her slow, mid-western way as she entered the kitchen. The screen door clattered like stones hitting concrete from behind her. She had just come home from her job as a dispatcher at the Upland Police Department. She was dressed in her work uniform, which consisted of a light blue blouse and a neatly pressed dark navy skirt. I was wearing my uniform as well – a faded Scorpions jersey that featured a howling mustachioed man covered in head bandages with metal forks scratching at his eyes. The bright red logo of the biggest heavy metal band to ever come out of Germany floated above his agonized face. The last rays of the setting sun had made their way past the white birch tree in the front yard and through the kitchen window. The muffled daily sounds of laughter, teenage profanity and the rusty song of the swings that sagged from the bird feces covered backyard swing-set laced the air.

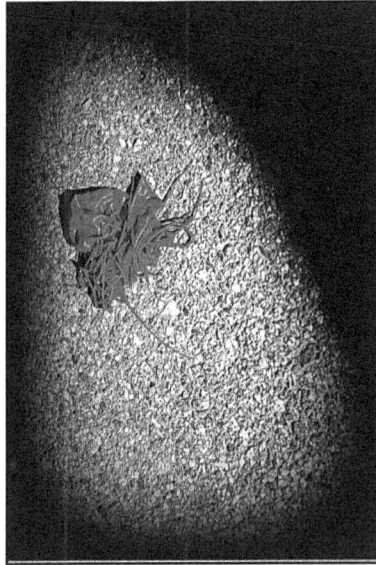

I could feel the coldness of the linoleum crusted kitchen floor on the soles of my bare feet as the wind chimes outside gently rattled and swayed. A rerun of *Barney Miller* buzzed in from the side den that had been taken over by shag carpeting the color of a Day-Glo swamp. "Did you ever wonder why the sperm whale, which is the largest mammal on the face of the earth, has a throat about that size?" a disheveled and exasperated Barney told his precinct as he formed a small circle, the size of a quarter with his thumb and fingers. "…Because that's the way it is. And there ain't anything you can do about it."

Did I know a girl named Anna Marie Bachoc? It seemed like such a random question for my mom to be throwing out there. I had never let on to my mom about the crush I had on Anna throughout Junior High. No way I would have ever even mentioned her name in front of her. I shudder to think of the gentle chiding that would have followed if I had. "So, tell me a little more about this Anna Marie. You're blushing. I bet she's cute."

Did I know a girl named Anna Marie Bachoc?

The answer was yes.

Anna and I shared the same homeroom back at Upland Junior High. The only break fate had bestowed upon me during the 7th grade was to drop me in the same homeroom as Anna. The homerooms at Upland Junior High were assigned alphabetically by last name. So maybe it wasn't fate that brought us together so much as it was the alphabet.

Anna was royalty as far as my retainer-fitted, KISS obsessed, comic book loving misfit self was concerned. To be acknowledged by her was to be temporarily lifted out of teenage peasant-dom where a good day was any day where you didn't get body-slammed into the hallway lockers between class by some future warehouse worker as he'd laugh and make sure to bellow out loud enough for everyone to hear "next time get out of my way ya dink."

Anna was an unknowing buoy that helped keep me afloat in these merciless waters. I clung to the Fridays where she'd be sure and remind me to have a good weekend. The Monday mornings where she'd ask how my weekend had gone. And the every once in awhile where she'd chide me for seemingly having "a different KISS T-shirt for every day of the week." None of these moments probably meant a whole lot of anything to her. But to me her smile was a glass of cold water in a sweltering desert of social rejection.

Anna, like me, was Catholic. Though she was far better at it than I was. My devotion to the faith was limited to attending mass every Sunday at St Joseph's and going to Catechism every Wednesday night where I'd waste the hour trying to discreetly read the latest issue of *The Incredible Hulk* I'd tucked inside my Catechism reader as the elderly and constantly scowling Sister Lucy went on and on and on about guilt, sin, suffering and salvation in her thick Irish accent. "He died, so that you might have life everlasting. I want you to let that sink in." Perhaps, it wasn't me she was looking at when she said that through her clenched yellow teeth, but it always felt like it was.

Every now and then Sister Lucy would break up the monotony of the liturgies by gripping a cherry wood ruler with double metal edges and wielding it across the bare knuckles of the unbelievers and those unfortunate souls caught smuggling Marvel Comics contraband inside their Catechism readers.

I doubt Anna's knuckles ever felt the cherry wood sting of a Sister's ruler. Anna was an active member of St. Margaret Mary's parish. She was no doubt as familiar with the Apostles' Creed as I was with issue #121 of *The Amazing Spider-Man*—a seminal issue where Gwen Stacey, Peter Parker/Spider-Man's blue-eyed, blonde haired, purple headband wearing high school sweetheart, comes to a tragic end at the hands of the Green Goblin. Anna had no time for Gwen Stacey and the Green Goblin. By the time she was 15 she was assisting in teaching and shepherding the youngest of lambs at St. Margaret Mary's parish and familiarizing them with the Apostles' Creed.

I believe in the Holy Spirit … the communion of saints, the forgiveness of sins, the resurrection of the body, and the life everlasting.

"Oh yeah, Anna," I wistfully answered my mom as I gently placed the orange back down onto the paper towel. It was good hearing her name. It was like hearing a favorite song I hadn't heard in forever.

It'd been awhile. I had not seen Anna since we both got our reprieves from that cramped Upland Junior High homeroom some three years earlier. Like my older sister who proceeded me and my younger brother who would follow me I was transferred and bused 5.1 miles south of Upland to Montclair High whose official school colors were fittingly black and blue. Some of my Junior High classmates would use a relative's address to avoid being sent into the "dangerous" waters of Montclair High. I had no such concerns. The silver lining to be an outsider looking in is that you exist inside a crater and you are impervious to things like your outside surroundings.

As I migrated south Anna ascended to become an Upland High Highlander. It seemed pre-ordained that our worlds would wind up spinning in opposite directions after unexpectedly colliding. We existed in two different orbits. I was Arnold Horshack in black plastic granny glasses. And Anna mirrored the enigmatic model from the Night Ranger "Sister Christian" video. Smiling in slow motion floating down a foggy campus hallway in a flowing graduation gown with a power ballad breathing down her neck.

"I know Anna," I answered my mom. "We shared the same home

room back at Upland Junior High. She's pretty great."

My mom took a long, hesitant drag from her cigarette and blew the smoke towards the kitchen window screen. Her shoulders started to sag. Something wasn't right. I could tell by her body language that she was hoping I hadn't had a connection. Not for her sake, but for mine.

She paused for a short eternity.

"I'm sorry."

"Sorry?"

"They found her body yesterday…"

My mom took another drag. As a single mom working 40 hours a week she was always achingly tired when she arrived home from work. But this was a different kind of tired. A dusty, spiritual kind of tired I'd never seen her wear before. I didn't want to make eye contact. I instead stared down into the abyss of the Pine-Sol scented kitchen tiles. *They found her body yesterday.* Everything inside me froze.

"They what … ?"

"They found her yesterday … in an orange grove off 23rd Street."

"What?"

My mom's next words sputtered and buzzed inside my head like a cold, bloodless radio frequency fading in and out.

"suspect is ex-boyfriend … lured her into a garage … said he just wanted to talk … pulled an extruded plastic electrical cord from behind his back, looped it around her neck several times and viciously tugged … it was instant … asphyxiation … they found her body in a freshly dug grave … That's all I know right now honey. That's all anybody knows. I wish there was something more … "

There wasn't.

I stood soundless and frozen for a 30 second eternity. All I could give was a passive nod in my mother's direction. If there is one unwritten rule for insecure 17-year-old-males it is NEVER openly weep in public. To do so is a social misdemeanor. To openly weep in front of your mother is to turn that misdemeanor into an unpardonable felony.

"I'm sorry honey. I'm sorry. You want to talk about it? … maybe not right now … maybe later."

I squeaked out a fractured "maybe later."

My mom, who was not the touchy-feely type, leaned in and gave me an extended maternal embrace. As soon as she released me I darted off like a freshly fired cannonball to the family bathroom and began the process of stringing myself back together one slow, deep breath and one cold, slap of water to the face at a time. I had lost grandparents and distant relations in my 17 years but nothing like this. Up until this moment death had been an abstract. It was something distant and unreal. Something I'd contextualized and understood through the yellowed 4 color panels of a dog-eared reprint of *Spider-Man* #121.

"I'm going to get you Goblin! I'm going to destroy you slowly … and when you start begging for me to end it … I'm going to remind you of

one thing ... You killed the woman I love ..."

I continued blubbering as the cold water continued streaming from the bathroom faucet. I did my best to not look up at my quivering lip, nose sniffling, and puffy-eyed reflection. But like Lot's wife I couldn't help but look. And just like Lot's wife I turned to a pillar of salt upon doing so. I clenched my eyes tighter and tried to escape the encroaching shadows by temporarily imagining the water dialing down the drain was the soothing sounds of waves crashing down on a distant peaceful shore.

I was able to temporarily get my troubled mind to distract itself by focusing on Van Halen's "Ain't Talking Bout Love." I stitched myself together enough to make it to the dinner table where I immediately got into a staring contest with the microwaved bean and cheese burrito that lay atop the thin paper plate like a beached whale. I took two half-hearted bites of the lukewarm microwaved Rosarita refried bean-filled tortilla in the hope that it would fill the indefinable empty lingering inside. But it was all for naught. There was just too much empty to fill.

"I'll finish later," I said tucking the burrito into a paper towel and slowly backing away from the table. "Just not now."

And then I fled to the place where I always fled for solace—inside the carefully organized and curated record crates that lined the bedroom walls. A thick, clear plastic sleeved fortress of solitude. I thumbed through the alphabetized, 12-inch cardboard jungle desperately seeking an antidote to the poison coursing through my system. The records only seemed to echo and mock my loss: The Beatles *HELP!*, Marvin Gaye *What's Goin On*, Motley Crue *Too Fast For Love* … Pink Floyd *Dark Side of the Moon*. Perfect.

My still trembling fingers gently touched the needle down onto the black spinning grooves. I grabbed the small brown plastic waste bucket plastered with a peeling sticker of local hair metal band Steeler and a handful of light blue Kleenex. And then I plunged onto my bed, silently wept and clung to the beige pillow as if it were a life preserver as the melancholy orchestrations Pink Floyd spiraled on.

And just when I thought I had gotten it all out I realized I hadn't. More deep breaths. More silent sobbing. Another light blue Kleenex. I was an amateur when it came to the process of grieving. And now the training wheels were off. I was wobbling, and shaking and desperately trying to maintain my balance.

The handful of Kleenex I'd brought with me was spent. I was reduced to wiping the sleeve of the Scorpions *Blackout* tour jersey across the snotty, teary contours of my face. I rose up from the bottom bunk and flipped the timeworn copy of *Dark Side of the Moon* over and grabbed another handful of Kleenex.

What kind of universe was it that would extinguish the life of a 17-year-old girl without reason?

The room grew darker. My mind swayed faster. The tide of tears continued to rise and recede. Rise and recede. The brown plastic waste bucket covered with the peeling stickers transformed into a landfill of mucus filled tissue as Pink Floyd's *Dark Side of the Moon* kept spiraling.

"I am not frightened of dying. Any time will do: I don't mind. Why should I be frightened of dying? There's no reason for it – you've got to go sometime … there is no dark side of the moon, really. As a matter of fact it's all dark."

Anna Marie Bachoc, 17, of Upland, California was taken much too soon on Friday, April 22. A victim of homicide.

Ms. Bachoc was a senior at Upland High School and was scheduled to graduate in June.

A memorial fund has been set up with the Saint Margaret Mary parish youth group where Ms. Bachoc had been active and was a religion class teacher.

Family and friends may pay their respects at a rosary prayer service 4 to 7 p.m. Monday, and again 8:45 to 9:15 a.m. Tuesday, at Saint Margaret Mary Parish.

She is survived by her parents, Raymond and Margaret Bachoc; brother Martin, sisters Kathie, Marie, Marguerite and Jenny, and many lifelong friends and relatives.

The home of the Upland Highlanders is covered in thin sheets of collective grief. Anna's friends emotionally break down in the middle of Geometry. Those who didn't really know her find themselves covered by her shadow. The white tiled marked-up hallways are strung with stunned silence and shared memories. The morning cascades down in numbing slow motion. The echo of a somber homeroom announcement reminds students that there are counselors available for students in need of support in these most trying of moments should they need them.

No such announcements make their way to the shores of Montclair High. I am on my own to process her passing. Although I live in Upland my Upland address has been determined to be not "Upland enough" by the Gods of school district gerrymandering. Thus I have spent the last three years as a Montclair High Cavalier.

There are far fewer BMWs to be found in the student parking lot at Montclair High than there are at Upland High, but other than that, they share the same teenage fears and insecurities as any other high school on the map that you could care to toss a dart at while blindfolded.

There's an endless loop playing through my mind and I have no idea how to make it to stop: The loop begins with her distant voice *"You have a different KISS shirt for every day of the week, don't you?"* followed by her distinct laugh before bleeding into a mantra of—*Anna*. I want to know why. I want to know how come. I want Judas Priest's *Screaming for Vengeance* to politely leave my internal playlist …

Perhaps I could spill to my friends but the only things we tend to spill are pretty much limited to Iron Maiden and perhaps the latest issue of *The Avengers* or *Tomb of Dracula*. Besides, what can they do … and what can I do really outside of pumping up *Screaming for Vengeance* to eleven in my head another 2,000 times? And so there is only this:

"You alright?"

"Just tired."

"You sure?"

"Pretty sure."

"You seem different."

It was neither Christmas nor Easter but my lapsed Catholic soul contemplated the notion of going to St. Joseph's and finding a dusty, empty pew and send off a prayer to Anna—a tossed off Hail Mary in a bottle. *Hail Mary full of grace… I HATE "him" and hate myself for not pulling off some unknowable and nameless, heroic-type move that could have spared her … Amen.*

The cry of the coyotes has grown dimmer over the years. Their numbers have thinned with the invasion of each new housing tract and strip mall. Just the other day I saw an out of place stray whose ribs were practically puncturing through its ratted fur as it lightly pranced through a construction site in search of a distant place that existed now solely as a collective memory.

They found your mother's abandoned station wagon in a distant corner of a Vons parking lot. The Vons that was located in the northernmost area of Upland that distinguished itself from the rest of the city by demanding to be addressed by its more formal name "The San Antonio Heights." "The Heights" as the locals referred to it was the greenest, quietest, and most spacious patch the city of Upland had to offer. The Heights was most famous for the 35-foot, five-point star that one of the residents shone each holiday season and whose shine could be seen all across the Pomona Valley on even the coldest of twilights.

Your mother's station wagon sat there serenely in the supermarket parking lot largely unnoticed. It sat there for days stoically collecting dust amongst the dented shopping carts that nosily and squeakily rolled their way to the southernmost edge of the parking lot to retire.

The fact it was your mother's station wagon is a detail that makes it all ache that much more. A mother handing off the keys to the family car to their teen is an act of faith, a pivotal milestone for both parent and child. That defining moment where the parental foot comes slowly off the brake and the child's foot hits the gas. This is where the contract gets finalized, where adolescence is shed and the journey down the blind open highway towards an unforeseen yet promising future begins. This is the way that it has all been laid out. This is the basic structure. The way it's always been. But foundations can crack. Mountains can crumble. Leaving in their wake only piles of debris to be rummaged and sorted through.

When they discovered the station wagon your purse was still there tilted on its side atop the passenger seat. There were no hidden secrets or illuminating clues to be found inside the purse. There was only what one would expect to find inside a 17-year-old's purse—California Drivers License, Upland High student body card, lip gloss, a compact folding make-up mirror, peppermint flavored breath mints … everything seemed to still be there save for any cash the purse may have once contained. The discovery of the station wagon wasn't much but so far it was all that there was.

The keys to the station wagon would never be found. It's not all that difficult to deduce the fate of the keys. The safe bet being that the keys were nonchalantly tossed to a nearby vacant field where they were left to slowly rust and forever lost to the ages not to be seen again.

Our lives are puzzles. Small connecting pieces slowly pieced together to create a whole.

Not long after the discovery of the abandoned station wagon

authorities would come across her body in a shallow trench.

The local papers would cover the story sporadically in the months ahead. But only sporadically. It was a more graceful and less sensationalistic time. A time where things crashed quieter but receded and lingered longer.

The San Antonio Heights Vons where Anna's mother's station wagon was uncovered would be leveled in 2007 to make way for a senior living community. The infamous San Antonio Heights Christmas Star was destroyed in the 2003 Grand Prix fire but would be rebuilt from the ashes in 2007 as a community symbol of perseverance and resilience. The star would be a little smaller than the original and its glow wouldn't reach as far but its shine would be felt and observed every winter by those drifting by on a surrounding freeway.

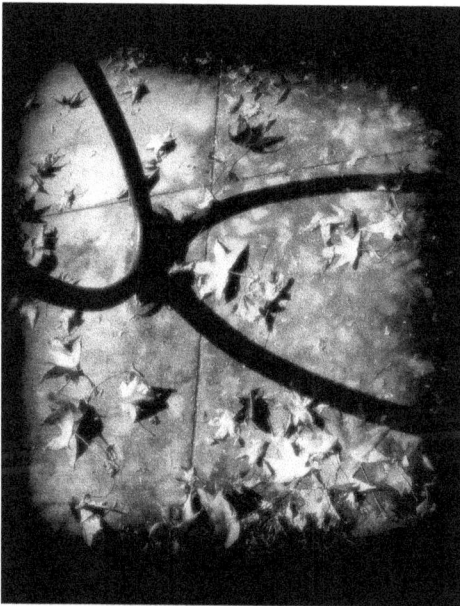

They say that anger and sorrow are two sides of the same coin. No, they're not. They are the same coin. They share the same nest. They are part of the same sensitive wound. A wound that heals but never closes. A wound easily re-aggravated. Rolling over in bed the wrong way, brushing against a hallway wall a little too closely, hearing a memory inducing melody come on from out of nowhere is to be unexpectedly reminded that the wound is still very much there and still very much a part of you.

I was now 19, no serious relationship on the horizon, working on a two-year associates degree that would end up taking roughly three times that long to attain, and drifting from one deadening low paying part-time strip mall job to an even more deadening low paying part-time strip mall job.

18-year-old Guilty of Murdering Ex-girlfriend

The newspaper article was maybe four paragraphs at best but I told myself it'd be best not to read it. What was the point? The only point was this—had she lived Anna would have no doubt been halfway through getting her bachelor's degree at the prestigious university of her choice on a full scholarship, at least halfway to being happily engaged and cementing the kind of future she deserved the kind that advertisers can only promise but never fulfill.

I stood alone in the frozen tundra of what she might have been and what I had become. All the transformative changes that are promised with the general admission entry ticket into one's twenties didn't seem to have gotten delivered to my address. Any noted changes to my existence seemed purely cosmetic at best. I was still in the place I'd always been despite some slight renovations to the landscape. The KISS posters were no longer tacked onto the walls, the comic books and *Mad* magazines had been unceremoniously replaced with Charles Bukowski novels and *SPIN* magazine and now resided in cardboard dog-eared boxes at one end of the narrow sliding door closet, and the record collection was now more Velvet Underground than Van Halen. The brown plastic trash can with the faded, peeling Steelers sticker had held on, lingering like a soldier who never got word that the war had long been over. The small suburban bedroom was a snake that had shed its skin but still retained its form and held all its ghosts in close.

18-year-old Guilty of Murdering Ex-girlfriend

I broke. I convinced myself there'd be some kind of closure to be found in the four paragraphs. There was no closure. There was only this: The electrical cord used in the killing was still wrapped around the body when they found it. A witness testified that they saw *him* driving Anna's mother station wagon the day of the murder without Anna and thought it was odd. A first-degree murder conviction was handed down.

I had gazed into the abyss. And true to form the abyss had gazed unblinkingly right back at me.

I avoid taking 11th Street past the old junior high with all it's dead weeds, cracked asphalt and scarred, crooked sidewalks.

But some days I forget.

Some days I can't help but look.

The place is exactly how I left it, only smaller.

Dead fields of abandoned lockers,

rusted basketball rims,

tetherballs swinging at half-mast

and the desperate strains of starving crows cawing at no one.

Swing down this way

When you're 17

Come seize all the free advice that you can tie

That we could have tied

That we could have tied

I never let her go.

Over 30 years later I remain haunted by the ghost of a 17-year-old girl I marginally knew for two years back in junior high. I continue to be followed by her echoes. They are found in the watching of reruns of David Lynch's *Twin Peaks* which centers on a town haunted by the elusive murder of Laura Palmer, a popular and pristine local high school girl, hearing the soft bruising tones of "Sister Christian" play on a Totally 80s Flashback Weekend and in the eyes of my niece who just recently celebrated her 17th birthday. The path can get so twisted.

It's said that there's an art to moving on and finding the strength and perseverance to push forward through loss and grief. There are two and a half crammed shelves at the library where I've worked for close to 15 years on this very subject. Books found under the Dewey Decimal call number of 155.937. Books with titles such as *Your Grief Your Way, The Grief Forest,* and *It's OK That You're Not OK: Meeting Grief and Loss in a Culture That Doesn't Understand.* I am constantly finding myself in the absurd position at my workplace

of directing people towards works on comfort and closure but somehow never making it there myself. 30-plus years on and here I am still trying to stumble past the anger, denial, and grief and push myself forward towards an acceptance that always appears to be so much closer than what it actually is.

In the early '90s I moved with my mom and stepdad to a new housing complex that had been built across the street from where Anna's seventeen-year-old body had been temporarily buried a decade prior. The site of her shallow grave had been transformed. The citrus groves that had once covered the area had given way to gated communities brimming with lemon scented air fresheners, depthless picture windows and small, curving streets with gentle, floral-scented names such as Oleander, Willow Jasmine, and West Sunset Curve.

For the longest time whenever I thought of Anna and myself in that dustbin of a homeroom there was only one of us I thought of as having ever been awkward, paralyzing insecure and embarrassedly unaware. Turns out we were both far more worthy and deserving than what we had convinced ourselves we were. A couple low hanging broken branches connected at the root trying to make it through the stages as best we could.

Egg.

Caterpillar.

Chrysalis.

~~Butterfly~~.

In the middle of writing all this down I had a soft focus dream.

The kind of dream that is simultaneously hazy and crystal clear. In the dream I was the age I am now and looked exactly how I had when my head had crashed to the pillow: a goatee streaked in gray, a few extra pounds than where I'm at when I'm at my best and thinning hair.

Anna fairs much better in the dream than I do. She looks exactly like she did in her high school yearbook photo – a smile, a beige sweater and a beaded necklace. She radiates.

"Hey you…" she warmly smiles as she gets in the old silver Toyota and adjusts the passenger seat. The sky is cloudless and blue. The highway before us is sunlit, endless and familiar. Anna and I are the only ones on it. We have no idea where we are going, or if we're ever going to get there.

Of course, I am happy to see her but I'm also achingly saddened. The dream feels real enough but I know when I wake she will be just as gone as she was before my head hit the pillow. I've read in more than a few different places that dreams are actually parallel universes that are every bit as real as the universe of the waking world. I'm not so sure how much I actually believe this but I do know that there's a very real part of me that'd like to believe it's true.

But who can say?

And who's to know?

Maybe existence is a mix tape that repeats on an endless loop. There is no reverse and there is no fast forwarding. No punching out the upper tabs and erasing or recording over any of it. It must

be listened to as a whole. Every awkward embarrassing off key moment, every drawn out verse, every joyous chorus and every heartbreaking outro must be listened to as it was intended.

Sister Christian, there's so much in life. Don't you give it up before your time is due ... you're motorin' ... you're motorin' ...

The next part of the dream has Anna turning to me and asking me in a concerned gentle tone if everything is ok. Her question hangs, floats and flutters. And then it lands like a crushing left hook to my skull. It knocks me further from the dream state and closer to the cold canvas of present reality. There are a thousand different ways I can answer her question. The possibilities are a bottomless pit. I could give her a half-hearted "Everything is fine." I could wearily close my eyes, shake my head side to side as I silently reach for the radio to elbow out the silence, or I could be honest and break both our hearts by letting all that I've been carrying inside explode across the dashboard like a can of shaken carbonated soda.

I don't answer her.

I really don't want to.

All I want is for us to stay on the highway and for us to be granted a little while longer to bask in the sun and the breeze, to be free and forgiven from all whom trespasses against us.

"Everything ok?" she asks again.

"Everything is ok Anna," I answer. I avoid looking her in the eye. "God, it's so good seeing you again. So good. You don't even know. You will never know."

We trail off into the horizon.

And then the dream it ends.

I awake gasping and shaken beneath a rumpled comforter. I stare up and try to find connections in the countless shadowy patterns to be found on the ceiling. The alarm will be going off in a few hours. And the sun will be rising over a fresh new cycle. There is no use in trying to get back to sleep. No use in trying to get back.

In the quad at Upland High School there lies a plaque with this inscription:

Ana Marie Bachoc - November 28 1965 – April 22 1983.

It is covered in leaves in the fall.

Pelted by rains in the winter.

... Scorched by the sun in the summer.

... and covered in blossoms each spring.

34

Acknowledgments

Special thanks to Keren Dancerette and Maritza Ocampo for their invaluable feedback.

Dennis Callaci for his support, love and guidance.

Mark Givens for putting this all in motion.

Buzzsaw for reaching out to me with his beautiful, melancholy and majestic photos.

About the Author

Allen Callaci is the lead singer for the band Refrigerator, an adjunct professor at Mt SAC Community College, and a librarian at the Rancho Cucamonga Public Library where he is the proud co-founder of the library's Star Wars Day—the largest Star Wars library event on the West Coast. He is also a freelance writer whose work has appeared in *MungBeing*, the *Poly Post*, *The Huffington Post*, *BKNation*, *Cinefantastique,* and various zines in the '90s. His memoir *Heart Like a Starfish* was released in 2016 on Pelekinesis. He hails from the Inland Empire region of Southern California.

BAMBOO
DART
PRESS

112 N. Harvard Ave. #65
Claremont, CA 91711

chapbooks@bamboodartpress.com
www.bamboodartpress.com

www.ingramcontent.com/pod-product-compliance
Lightning Source LLC
Chambersburg PA
CBHW081652270326
41933CB00018B/3446